MONEY IS LOOKING FOR YOU

The Secret Principles of Attracting Unlimited MONEY into Your Life.

EMMAN ROBERTS

TABLE OF CONTENTS

INTRODUCTION 1

CHAPTER 1: POVERTY 9

CHAPTER 2: YOU DON'T HAVE TO BE POOR 13

CHAPTER 3: VISUALIZATION 16

CHAPTER 4: THE POWER OF WORDS 20

CHAPTER 5: N-WORD'S ABOUT MONEY 27

CHAPTER 6: THE SUBCONSCIOUS MIND (HEART) 30

CHAPTER 7: FAITH AND BELIEFS 35

CHAPTER 8: GRATITUDES/PRAISES/THANKSGIVING 39

CHAPTER 9: MONEY AFFIRMATIONS 44

CHAPTER 10: CONCLUSION 49

ABOUT THE AUTHOR 52

ABOUT THE BOOK 53

REFERENCES 54

Emman Roberts Enterprise

#97078

Würzburg

Bayern

Germany

For more information contact:

Phone: +49-176-24551954

Social Media:

Facebook: psychology of Money

Personal page: Emman Roberts

Email: emmanroberts777@gmail.com.

ISBN-13: 978-9-69-229291-7

Cover Design by: jeweldsign

Printed in United States of America

Compiled by: Adefisan Adebola

Library Of Congress Control Number: 2022901863

INTRODUCTION

This is not a book to be read once and dumped on the bookshelf but a book to be read again and again, to fully understand the modus operandi of the **PRINCIPLES OF SUCCESS, PROSPERITY, AND ABUNDANCE OF MONEY** as instructed, well written, and explained in this book. In writing this awesome book; I assumed and believed that the reader of this great volume will be motivated by following this procedure:

Read, ponder, apply and use "the principles" stated in this book diligently, habitually, and consistently for your benefit.

The author called these incredible concepts **"SECRETS"** of attracting **MONEY** because the author boldly believed in the "principles" that are intelligently stated in this book after using the same principle to enrich himself individually and the people around him.

I decided to share these secret principles of **WEALTH, SUCCESS**, and **ABUNDANCE** of money to the readers, to people that desire more money, and to the ones who want to have a very good relationship with money so they can draw more it into their experience and enjoy more of it.

You can drastically improve your financial circumstances and monetary conditions by manifesting more financial freedoms into your life if you dare study this volume diligently and apply the principles of prosperity, success, and abundance of money as explained and shared here in this Book.

The first secret to be revealed to you inside this book about your accumulation of material **MONEY** or **WEALTH** and abundance of money **begins foremost in your MIND** before you can see it in your pockets, wallets, and bank accounts.

Read along and enjoy the ride and let us dive deeper into the secret of success, prosperity, and abundance of money. I will suggest that you have a note journal in writing down and taking notes of "**The Principles**" stated here in the book.

Read again and again, ponder, apply, and more applications. Reading tons of books on **WEALTH/MONEY** consciousness is very informative, likewise very good but one must apply these awesome principles to get the results you're seeking.

Always remember that "**KNOWLEDGE IS POWER**" if properly used and applied. Knowledge correctly applied and used makes a man unfit to be a slave to money and ignorantly **POOR** lacking material money.

This is a **Money consciousness Book** and it's strictly for the people who are interested in attracting more money into their respective lives utilizing and using their consciousness positively and correctly.

This is not a **GET RICH QUICK SCHEME**, an "*Abracadabra*" theory book that's going to deliver a billion dollars into your laps in a few minutes without practically applying "**THE PRINCIPLES**" of success, money, and wealth stated in book. You have to diligently practice and apply the "**The Principles**" before getting awesome results. "Wisdom is the principal thing; therefore, in all thy getting, get wisdom and understanding".

THE FIRST LAW OF HEAVEN

"As he thinketh in his heart (subconscious mind), so is he". That's the law that determines everything we are constantly experiencing as conditions in life. Things just don't happen to us as conditions in this awesome universe of ours. Everything happens according to **the law of consciousness.**

Our words, thoughts, and beliefs are **causes** and conditions are the **effects** according to the nature of our beliefs. The principles of **WEALTH** and **SUCCESS** work for everyone apparently; it does not care about your race, creed or color, neither does it care if you live anywhere around the World.

"IT WORKS IF YOU WORK IT".

MONEY WANTS YOU

"Money answers all things" (Eccl.10:19).

"Remember the Lord your God (source of supplies; Gift and the Giver) for it is he who gave you Power to get Wealth" (Deut.8:18).

Money is such a broad topic and subject that it could fill millions of pages, but after reading hundreds of books on wealth and prosperity, I decided to summarize my personal experiences. After many hours of reading and using these **SECRET PRINCIPLES** in my own life, I discovered that they perform wonders in my wallets and bank accounts. I am now going to share these "**PRINCIPLES**" with you, my readers.

Money is a medium of exchange and a **SUBCONSCIOUS BELIEF** in the mind and consciousness of the rich and wealthy and so also is **POVERTY**. The thought-image of money is the first principle to be observed and applied before you can draw more money into your experience.

The thought-image of **WEALTH** in your mind is the first cause relative to money and riches in the unseen realms before it appears as your outside visible realities. The mind is where the real action is if you are trying to manifest money and whatever it is you truly desire.

"And be not conformed to this world: but be ye transformed by the renewing of your mind" (Romans 12:2).

Acquiring an abundance of money and wealth always starts in your mind. *"It is impossible to impregnate your subconscious mind with the ideas of wealth and be poor".*

The secret of a blessed and prosperous man (mind) is found in 1ˢᵗ Psalm:

"Blessed is the man(mind) that delight and meditates on the laws of the lord day and night; he is like a tree planted by the rivers which yields fruits in its season and whatever he does shall prosper" (Psalm 1:2-3).

"THE ECONOMY OF THOUGHT" "Matters (conditions) do not matters; only **THE MIND** matters".

Your lack of money is always traceable to the fact that you have been seeking your supplies from a secondary source instead of God (source of supplies); the giver and the gift of all blessings including an abundance of money and all you truly desire.

AFFIRM: "I cannot be separated from God the source, giver and the gift".

Since we all knew money to be "The medium of exchange", everyone desires an abundance of money to live a happy and fulfilling life full of infinite blessings in this material world we live in.

Trying to create money from the place of lack with such words as "I need or I want" is not being in alignment with the source of supplies(God) because God (Source) is **"I AM"** and not **"I will be"**. You should always affirm and verbalize the goods you desire in the present tense such as *"I AM WEALTHY" "I AM RICH"*.

NOTE: *"The Lord (Source) makes Poor or Rich; he brings Low and lifted" (Samuel 2:7).* It is easy for God to make you Rich and Wealthy just as he grows a blade of Grass.

AFFIRM: "My money grows like grass".

Your attitudes towards money will either attract or repel money from you. Poverty, lack, limitations, and shortage of money in your life are nothing but the by-products of wrong penury thoughts, words, and beliefs that are deeply embedded in your subconscious mind but they can be easily erased by speaking, thinking, and believing right prosperity concepts about money. The knowledge that God is your source of supplies made you unfit to be poor and live in penury.

NOTE: "Your prosperity and abundance of Money do not depend on others or the economy or wherever you are in the universe and in every coin of the realms". People and things may be your channels but God is your only source of supplies; whatever it is you truly desire, go to God (THE SOURCE).

Seek ye first the kingdom of God and his righteousness and all these things (material things inclusive) shall be added unto you"(Matt.6:33).

"MONEY WANTS YOU"

CHAPTER 1: POVERTY

"Poverty is but a sleep of wealth". "The destruction of the poor is their poverty" (Proverbs 10:15). Meaning their poverty words, thoughts, ideas and beliefs have placed them in abject poverty.

A poor person thinks and believes poverty thoughts. There is no nobility in poverty; it is a disease of the mind. A wealthy man once said "I have been poor and I have been rich but rich is better", same as the author; "Rich is always better in all ramifications".

AFFIRM: Poverty is no good to me.

Poverty is more often in the mind than in your pocket books, wallets, and bank accounts. You have dominion over money but why are you walking around poor and living in abject poverty and penury? Exercise your God- given power over material money so you can enjoy more money abundantly. Most are poor due to their ignorance of not knowing how **THE LAW OF THE MIND** operates in order to have all the goods they truly desire.

"My people are destroyed for the lack of knowledge" (Hosea 4:6).

Many people in abject poverty do not know that "The inside mirrors the outside"; "As within, so without"; "As in subconscious mind, so as conditions and life experiences".

NOTE: "IGNORANCE equals HARDSHIP and POVERTY" "POVERTY is the root of **ALL EVIL"**

"There are no Mountains anywhere; every man's ignorance is his mountain". If any man can get wealthy by constructive thinking through the use of their mind, then you can as well use and apply all these **PRINCIPLES OF WEALTH AND SUCCESS**. "We are all born with a built- in-Greatness; find yours in your mind". The law of prosperity and acquisition of wealth is just, exact and impartial and it's no respecter of persons; it works the same for everyone.

Famine, economic crisis, recession, thinking there is a shortage of money in the universe or that the evil wealthy folks in the world took all the available money are not your problems and they are not the truth as well because there is no shortage of money in this abundant universe of ours.

You don't lack money, what you lack are ideas on how to attract money. If you keep feeding your mind with prosperity thoughts, ideas, and beliefs, your financial problems are going to disappear and you will begin to attract riches into your experience if you dare to apply these principles as stated in the book. Our realities follow our beliefs and according to every man's beliefs, it is done unto him because a man is but his beliefs expressed and consciousness objectified".

Most people are always criticizing money but are still working hard to get it, not knowing that you cannot attract what you are resenting and criticizing. **Always make friends with money** and you will always have plenty of it. We are living in the universe of **"Causes and Effects"**. Thoughts and beliefs are the causes and conditions are the effects.

"There are no poor people; there are only people who do not know the riches of God within them" (paraphrasing Rev. Ike). "If **you want to be Rich; watch what the POOR do, and don't do it**" (Rev. Ike)

The fear of POVERTY is his greatest power; you have to be ruthless with the ideas of poverty in your mind if you want to be **RICH, SUCCESSFUL**, and **WEALTHY**.

"I can't help the poor if I am one of them; so I get rich and give back to me that`s a win-win" (jay z).

Poverty is no bar to Greatness; for poverty can be removed by the right thoughts, ideas, and beliefs.

AFFIRM: "I cast the burden of POVERTY on God-within and go free".

Magnetize your mind with these ideas of success, prosperity, and abundance of Money and you shall never lack Money and all Goods you truly desire.

"POVERTY IS NO GOOD TO ME"

CHAPTER 2: YOU DON'T HAVE TO BE POOR

God Almighty (Source of all blessings) did not create you to be poor. God wants you to be rich, prosperous, and be in good health even as your soul prospers. *"Beloved, I pray that you prosper in all things and be in health, even as your soul prospers (John3:2).*

Wealth and poverty; success or failures; All begins in the mind before it appears as conditions in your outer realities. Material money you possessed or lacks are all reflections of your state of mind and consciousness. Nothing is ill-fated or predestined in the universe of causes and effects. Every condition is first formed in the mind... **"THE COSMIC LAW OF THE MIND"** *states... As a man (mind) thinks in his heart (subconscious mind); so is he (Proverbs 23:7).*

Just as people learned to be poor; they can **UNLEARN POVERTY** and learn how to be prosperous. I am reminded of the famous quote by one of the authors money conscious mentors...Rev. Ike "there are no POOR people; only people who are not aware of the riches of God within them". That's an awesome true profound statement.

No man is kept in poverty because opportunities have been taken away from him. THOUGHTS and IDEAS are the only power that produces tangible riches and wealth. You can prosper regardless of your conditions and the world economic conditions.

NOTE: Ideas make millionaires and billionaires. If you talk and believe in lack of money; you will get lack of money and poverty and likewise, if you talk plenty and abundance of money; you will get more abundance of money.

You deserve an abundance of money and plenty because of the simple reason that you are a loving child of God (source of supplies) and this is the truth of everyone born into this world. Lack of money and poverty might be a fact as your condition presently but the truth of you is wealth and abundance if you know who you are and the power of God in you.

"In the image and the likeness of God" (source) you are created and God gave you dominion over everything on earth including material money; exercise your birthright as a loving child of God and stop crawling in **POVERTY. THINK RICH, FEEL RICH,** and **START WALKING IN THE ABUNDANCE** that is all around you.

"GOD WANTS YOU TO BE RICH"

"THE CONSCIOUSNESS OF WEALTH PRODUCES WEALTH"

CHAPTER 3: VISUALIZATION

Where there is no vision, the people perish
(Proverbs 29:18).

"Visualization is deliberate dreaming your **VISION** (desires) into physical manifestations by imagining yourself in your mind exactly the way you wanted to be, do and have it in the nowness of consciousness".

"Visualization is deliberately seeing and dreaming things that do not yet exist in your world into existence in the secret theatre of your mind like they already exist" and it shall surely appear as physical realities in your world as conditions.

Visualization is forming a "*MENTAL IMAGE*" in your mind thereby impressing your subconscious mind with the mental image which the subconscious is going to express out as physical realities (Conditions). Whatever is impressed on the subconscious mind persistently is going to be manifested as your outside realities; as within, so without; as above, so below; as in the Subconscious mind; so as Conditions.

Visualization is one of the fastest and most effective **"MIND POWER"** method principles to get what you truly desire and want, if it's appropriately mastered and correctly done; it's one of the most effective **MIND POWER** we all possess. Experience in "IMAGINATION" what you would love to experience as physical realities in your mind.

Using your imaginary **VISION/MIND** eyes; the esoteric eyes of God within; Sight, Touch, Smell and Taste) during your visualization prayers treatment. These Techniques fasten it up to get quick results; it's a spiritual sensation that goes beyond an intellectual exercise in the (3D WORLD); third physical dimension. *"As far as your eyes can see, it shall be given unto you (Genesis 13:14)"*

See yourself in your mind as you desire to be and what you see in your visualization exercise will manifest in your physical realities as Conditions and Life experiences; what you see is what you will get. Do not coerce or force mental pictures in your mind during visualization. Visualization should be easily and effortlessly done without any coercion and any type of force needed or necessary; it is meant to be enjoyed with Ease, Comfort, Joy, and Love.

Using the state of Akin to sleep where no effort is required during your visualization **PRAYERS** treatments because the subconscious mind (The great within) is more fertile in a drowsy state before dripping off to sleep or upon waking up from sleep. The subconscious mind can be easily fooled and impregnated with visualization because the subconscious cannot distinguish between what is real and mental picture in the theatre of your mind.

The subconscious mind can be easily impressed upon when the Conscious reasoning mind is in **AMBIENCE**; The state of suspension or a drowsy state before retiring to bed and upon waking up (Alpha state) when the Conscious mind is receptive and quiet. Then the Power of the subconscious rises and record whatsoever is impressed upon it just like a movie scene and play it back to you in the physical realm as your conditions.

Anything that you can see yourself becoming, doing, and having in your visualization exercise; you will surely become because it is the nature of the subconscious mind to reproduce back to you whatever is impressed upon it, either Good, Bad, or indifferent.

NOTE: "What you see is what you get" (VISUALIZATION).

Always think, speak, believe, and envision unlimited money and not lack money in your visualization **PRAYER'S** treatments if you dare to prosper and enjoy an abundance of money.

TIPS ON VISUALIZATION: - Never go to sleep without visualizing whatever you truly desire in your mind (Good health, Prosperity, Success, Love, Happiness, and Unlimited Money).

I'll love to end this visualization chapter with flip Wilsons' words, *"What you see (VISION) is what you get"*.

"WHAT YOU SEE IS WHAT YOU GET OUT OF LIFE".

CHAPTER 4: THE POWER OF WORDS

There are no idle words either spoken, written, thoughts, or inner conversations:

- ♦ Words are bonds.
- ♦ Words are magic.
- ♦ Words are spells.
- ♦ Words are Incantations.
- ♦ Words are an extension of thoughts.
- ♦ Words are creative.
- ♦ Words are spirit.
- ♦ Words are divine.

The power of spoken words is one of the greatest gifts that God almighty (Source) has bestowed on men; he does not give it to the animals or plants. Words are the most powerful weapon we humans possessed. *"In the beginning, was the word and the word was with God and word was God (Source)" (John 1:1).*

God almighty put creative words in your mouth and it is your power to exercise your God-given creative power (words) wisely, positively, and correctly to bless instead of cursing yourself. Your words are your almighty power because your word is God itself.

By your words, you are justified (Blessings) and by your words, you are condemned (Cursed) (Mathew 12:36).

In the beginning, was the word and not conditions. God put creative words in your mouths so you can speak your conditions and Life experiences into physical Manifestation. And the words became flesh and registered in your life as conditions. Your word becomes incarnate as your feelings then transform to your conditions.

As you are verbalizing your words either silently, spoken, written, or through inner conversations, you are prophesying your future and surely you are going to meet your words as a condition in a due course. *"Even though the tongue is a small part of the body, but what enormous damage it can cause" (James 3:5).*

Be careful what you are always verbalizing to yourself within your mind. I strongly believe that the tongue is the strongest organ in the human body. By your words, you are justified and condemned, it is a true statement. Before you witness any condition in your life it all begins with your word. In the beginning, it was the word, not the conditions; it all started in your mouth.

The tongue of the wise is health, wealth, prosperity, and infinite money.

AFFIRM: "I bless my words; therefore, I bless my world".

Every thought and words are always the Causes and every condition are the Effects because as a man thinks, so is He. Never say anything you don't want to experience to yourself. Never say **'I am poor'**, **'I am broke'**, **' I am penniless'**. Remember the verse:

"Let the poor say I am rich" (Joel 3:10).

"So tell them as surely as I live, declared the lord, I will do to you the very things I heard you say, " (Numbers 14:28).

Words are seeds and when dropped to the invisible spiritual realms. They grow and bring forth after their respective kinds. Your words create your feelings and your feelings invariably let the blessings according to the nature of your words, thoughts and beliefs. Man is bound, enslaved, and set free by the words of his mouth. Those who speak little get little and likewise those who speak abundance of money and plenty are rewarded with abundance and plenty of money.

The law of prosperity and money is just, impartial, exact, and works for everyone the same and it is no respecter of persons, creed, race, or color. Our words are a double edge sword. Our words are the wall of papers of the mind and our magical incantation. Our word casts a spell and becomes the conditions of our lives.

We think our words into existence through linguistic constructions and our world is modified by our words. To keep talking and believing '**POVERTY**' and expecting to be '**RICH**' is to play a fool's game because what you say and believe about yourself is what you get out of life. It cannot be otherwise, because as a man (MIND) think, speaks, and believes so he is. *Death and life are in the power of the tongue (Proverbs 18:21),* which makes us responsible for what we are verbalizing and believing about our self.

You cannot talk lack of money and expect abundance. Your life moves according to the direction of your own **WORDS** and **BELIEFS** about yourself. Your tongue is the pen of a ready writer, if you have poor words and believes about yourself you will have poor living conditions.

Turn your mouth around by talking and believing in the riches of life that are all around you. You cannot talk about how bad the drought is and attract the rain. You cannot talk about poverty and attract an abundance of money. If you have a poor mouth you are going to have poor living conditions. *'The tongue of the wise is health' (Proverbs 12:18).*

NOTE: Always remember these words whenever you are speaking lack and poverty words to yourself:

1. My words will not return to me void,
2. My words will not return to me empty,
3. My word always produces fruits.

"So shall my word be that goes forth out of my mouth, it shall not return unto me void but it shall accomplish that which I sent it"(Isiah55:11).

Even the master-mind (Jesus Christ) said, *'He shall have whatsoever he said' (Mark 11:23),* both riches and poverty is an offspring of your own words and beliefs". There are no idle words because every word has power either you are ignorant of the power of spoken words or not.

Either you speak them consciously or unconsciously; you shall surely eat the sweet or bitter fruits of your own words. If you do not consciously know that your words are creative and have powers affecting your life conditions, you are missing out on some amazing knowledge. Your word **PROPHESIES** your future according to the nature of your **WORDS** and **BELIEFS.**

"The words that I speak are spirit and they are life" (John 6:63).

Words are mental equivalent (Beliefs) which produces their image and likeness not only in our bodies but in our financial affairs as well. "Words are the most powerful drugs used by mankind" (Rudyard Kipling). Words are the coin of heaven and money is the earthly manifestation, words will enrich or make you poor according to how you are using them.

Use them positively and wisely. We breathe life into our world with our words. It is our beliefs in words that are creating our physical realities in this 3rd (Third Dimension) world.

Your words always go forth and prepare a place for you in the nearest future as your conditions. *"The stroke of the whip makes marks in flesh but the stroke of the tongue can break the bones". Life and Death are in the power of the tongue (Proverbs 18:21)*; use your almighty power of Words to bless your life and financial affairs instead of cursing your own life with poverty thoughts, words and Belief.

Make sure you are always casting Good spells (Gospel) on yourself in your Mind. Make sure you are casting Prosperity spells instead of Poverty spells on yourself through the power of your own Word.

NOTE: "What you say is what you get out of life", "in the beginning was the word and not conditions."

CHAPTER 5: N-WORD'S ABOUT MONEY

Never say bad 'WORDS' about MONEY; Money is very sensitive to your 'WORDS' and 'BELIEFS' about her on a psychic (psychological level). Always be careful about what you are saying and believing about money because money is clairvoyant and she always hears you; money has ears psychologically and spiritually. *'Thou art ensnared by the words of your mouth' (Proverbs 6:2).*

These are the 'WORDS' never to say about Money:

- Never say money is the root of all evil.
- Never say money is going to make you evil and be a bad person.
- Never say money is too hard to get.
- Never resent money.
- Never say the wealthy folks are evil.
- Never say money is filthy.
- Never deny money: if you deny money, money is also going to deny you.
- Never say money is going to corrupt you.
- Never disrespect money in any form.
- Never be a money hater.
- Never envy the wealthy folks: just be one of them.
- Never be afraid of money.

- Never say 'I don't have any money, let the poor say I am rich.
- Never use the word 'Spend Money'. Instead, circulate or use money because what you spend is gone forever but what you circulate returns back to you multiplied.

AFFIRM: 'All The Money I use and circulate returns back to me multiplied'.

NOTE: That's how you always get hold of your money, think of money as a personality; talk to money regularly, what you say and believe about money is what you get.

The majority of people kicks and talks money away from them instead of talking money to them by saying and affirming negative thoughts, words, and beliefs about money to themselves. Instead of saying such an aforementioned negative statement and words about money: Turn your mouth around and speak only lovely and harmonious words about money Such as the following:

- Money is wonderful.
- Money is freedom.
- Money is comfort.
- Money is power.
- Money is love energy.

28

- Money is great.
- Money is clairvoyant.
- Money supports my life.
- Money is Very good and there is nothing evil about money.

If you started having a positive outlook and belief about money; you will have a very good relationship with money and money is going to keep flowing into your life in abundance and you will start enjoying more money as much as you can. 'Saying and believing money is evil, will keep kicking money away from You'. That's a money rejection complex that keeps money away from lots of poor people.

FREE MONEY FROM ALL EVIL ACCUSATIONS

CHAPTER 6: THE SUBCONSCIOUS MIND (HEART)

As a man thinks in his Heart (Subconscious Mind) so is he and the conditions of his life (Proverbs 23:17).

As a man thinks, feels, and believes in his heart (Subconscious Mind) so is he and his life experience and conditions. This is one of the most profound statements in the holy bible stated by the richest king in the history of the bible (King Solomon) and this profound statement is also one of the author's favorite biblical verses.

Every conditions, circumstances, and life experiences are the out-picturing of our deep-seated beliefs in the subconscious area of the mind. Our thoughts, words, and deep-rooted beliefs impressed by the conscious mind into the subconscious mind are registered as feelings and therefore become our condition in outer-realities. **That is the word becoming flesh, *"And the Word was made flesh and dwell among us". (John 1:14).***

The subconscious mind is called '**THE HEART**' in the holy bible. It is a Chaldean word in ancient allegories. The Subconscious mind controls 96 to 97% of our life's condition according to science and everything that is happening in your life is as a result of your subconscious beliefs impressed by your conscious mind according to the nature of your thoughts and beliefs. That is the reason your thoughts and believes always become things (Conditions). *"Be careful what you think, because your thoughts run your life" (Proverbs 4:23).*

Whatever is impressed on your subconscious mind by thinking, feeling, and believing is automatically expressed on the outside as your conditions. That's the reason why you should be careful what you are saying or repeating to yourself in your mind because the subconscious mind is a silent listener recording everything you are verbalizing, thinking, and believing just like a tape recorder and then playing it back to you as your conditions and life experiences. *"Guard your Heart (Subconscious Mind) with all diligence because out of it are the issues of life" (Proverbs 4:23).*

Repetition is the language of the subconscious mind. What you think, feel, believe and keep repeating into your conscious mind are going to be impressed upon your subconscious mind either consciously or unconsciously, good, bad or indifferent; you are going to get a result as conditions according to the nature of your thoughts, words, and beliefs.

31

If you can successfully impress your subconscious mind with the idea of wealth and abundance of money you will be wealthy and have an abundance of money because *it is the nature of the subconscious mind to reproduce back to you whatever it is impressed upon it* and that's how the law of mind operates and it is no respecter of persons.

AFFIRM: "I am building the ideas of success and wealth into my subconscious mind now".

The subconscious mind is the seat of habits and that is the reason why you are always experiencing your subconscious beliefs as conditions. As you are habitually claiming your desires within your mind such as **"I AM RICH"**, you are under the compulsion to attract your claims subconsciously. Since 96% of our mental life is subconscious, those who are not aware of this great power within us all are missing and living ignorantly within the narrow limits.

The so-called "MIRACLES" that appear as physical realities and conditions are the children of the previous repetitions of words and believe that is impressed on the subconscious mind. Thoughts, words, and beliefs repeated over and over to self automatically impress the subconscious mind and thus becomes a feeling and once the feelings are formed in the subconscious it becomes our physical realities (conditions).

Every thought and word that is believed always makes a strong subconscious impression. *"People look at outward appearances but the Lord looks at 'THE HEART' (Subconscious Mind) " (1 Samuel 16:7).*

The frequent question always asked is **why do the rich get richer and the poor get poorer?**

It is because of different impressions given to the subconscious mind. Every day by their words, feelings, and beliefs; the rich are always affirming and repeating to themselves either consciously or unconsciously; **'I AM RICH'** and likewise the poor are always affirming and repeating to themselves 'I am broke/poor me' and it is subconsciously done unto every man according to their respective subconscious beliefs. **THE LAW OF LIFE IS THE LAW OF BELIEFS.**

Like a child born to a wealthy family, the child subconsciously feels and believes within him the idea of wealth in consciousness. His experience of wealth reinforces his feelings and beliefs of wealth which equates to his physical realities or the outer experience as conditions. Money is a subconscious vibration in the consciousness of the wealthy and so is poverty in the consciousness of the poor.

It is eternally true that the outside mirrors the inside, as within so without, as above so below, as in subconscious mind, so as conditions.

THE POWER TO ATTRACT AN ABUNDANCE OF MATERIAL MONEY IS IN YOUR SUBCONSCIOUS MIND, INVOKE FINANCIAL BLESSINGS INTO YOUR SUBCONSCIOUS MIND REGULARLY AND YOU WILL NEVER LACK MONEY OR BE BROKE.

CHAPTER 7: FAITH AND BELIEFS

"And according to your faith (BELIEF), be it unto you" (Matthew 9:20).

It is your words of faith that sets you free from poverty, lack, and limitations. When it comes to acquiring wealth and abundance of money, Faith builds up your courage and confidence thereby destroying fears and doubts regarding your money consciousness acquisition. Faith in God (Source) within you gives you dominion over every adversity, fear, poverty, and lack of money and all goods you truly desire. *"And Faith comes by hearing and hearing the word of God" (Romans 10:17).*

Faith unlocks the infinite storehouse within us all and connects us to the great within (God Within), the source of all blessings and abundance. There is a faith and there is a faith that moves mountains and this type of faith is expressed through our spoken words, thoughts, feelings, and beliefs accordingly. This type of unwavering faith transcends limitations, lack, and poverty. It expands our consciousness to be, do and have all the goods that we truly desire. *"But let him ask in faith, not wavering, for he that waver is like a wave of the sea driven with the wind and tossed" (James 1:6).*

Master your faith and you will automatically conquer doubts, fears, and every limiting idea about money. Fear is the most powerful of all thought forces but faith is the only remedy against unwanted fears.

NOTE: Fear isn't anything but shadows, *"God has not given us the spirit of fear, but of love, power and a sound mind" (Timothy 1:7).* Fear is man's worst enemy; it is faith turned upside down.

AFFIRM: "I release all fears about money and all money blocks in my subconscious mind now"

According to your faith, that's the law that determines everything. Faith and fear both demand you to believe in something you cannot see. Do you choose either faith or fear? riches or poverty? *"Choose you this day whom you serve" (Joshua 24: 15).*

You can choose to be poor or rich. It is a choice given to all of us born into this world and your choices determine your result concerning lack or abundance of money. It is done to every man according to his beliefs. Faith is what you believe and feel about yourself in your mind and the prevailing principle in the school of faith is *"He shall have whatsoever he said" (Mark 11: 23).*

We are to ask in faith and not doubting or wavering. If you do not believe that God (Source) is your instant and everlasting source of supplies and all abundance of blessings, you are going to be missing the point by limiting the abundance of money that is supposed to be coming to you. Faith is to believe what you do not see yet in physical realities but the reward of this unwavering faith is to see what you believe if you persevere. *"And without faith, it is impossible to please God (Source of Supplies) (Hebrew 11:6).*

"And if you could persevere and be patient you will be convinced that faith never fails" Just in a little while, the fruits will fall when its juice is full ". *"When the cloud is full of rain, they empty themselves upon the earth" (Ecclesiastes 11:3).*

Faith is resting on God's Words even though conditions deny your assumptions (Beliefs) and you find yourself in the chains of poverty due to ignorance of how the law of Prosperity operates. Faith is trusting God within contrary to the evidence of lack, limitations, and poverty which is now visible as your realities. *"The just shall live by faith" (Hebrews 10:38);* Loyalty to the unseen realities.

NOTE: Remember you can only see the result of your faith after it is completed, always exercise patience when trying to manifest money and all goods you truly desire with faith. Your Faith speeds up your manifestations of whatsoever goods you desire including money.

Faith is what gives our words and thought-forms in which we experience as conditions and physical realities. You have to believe it before you see it, that's a true statement. *"If thou can believe, all things are possible to him that believes" (Mark 9:23).* Your faith or beliefs is the hand of God (Source) molding the firmament into the image and likeness of which you believed.

There is an unwavering faith that transcends lack, limitations, and poverty. This is the kind of faith you must possess in consciousness to attract and draw more money into your experience. It can be done if you believe.

"ACCORDING TO YOUR FAITH/BELIEF,
THAT DETERMINES EVERYTHING
".

CHAPTER 8:
GRATITUDES/PRAISES/THANKSGIVING

"In everything, give thanks" (1 Thessalonians 5:18).

The first step to being great is being grateful. Gratitude and giving thanks for the money you already have is the law of increase and likewise complaining about the money you have is the law of decrease, lack, and limitations.

The fastest route to increase your finances (money) is through praises (Thanksgiving/ gratitude's) even before you physically see the money manifested as your physical reality in your 3D World (Third dimension world). Give thanks in advance for the money and financial abundance you truly desire and that's going to Turbo-change your abundance of money rushing towards you easily, quickly, and effortlessly.

Gratitude is the food of the soul (subconscious mind). Gratitude when expressed often attracts millions of new miracles and draws more money into your experience. Keeping a Gratitude journal is a must for you as a money- maker because a grateful heart is a constant magnet for miracles. Nothing new can come into your life unless you are grateful for what you already have including material possessions. To feel better about money, get into the act of emitting gratitude for the money that you already have and money that is on its way to you. Always invoke the act of gratitude for money and you will never be broke or lack money.

Lack and shortage of money most times come from lack of gratitude for the money you already have because gratitude is riches and complaint is poverty energetic wise.

An abundance of gratitude for money equals an abundance of money. Whoever has gratitude for money will be given more abundance of money and to the ungrateful, even the money he had shall be taken away from him and he shall be rewarded with nothing but poverty and empty pockets.

Gratitude is a great multiplier of money and giving thanks is always connecting us to the higher power within us all (God/Source), the source of our supplies, the giver, and the gift of all blessings. It is impossible to bring more money into your life if you are always complaining about a lack of money. All thoughts, words, emotions, feelings, and negative beliefs about money create more negative beliefs in your subconscious mind, thereby blocking more money from coming into your life.

Always train your mind to be attached to gratitude because gratitude is always a win-win, no matter what conditions you are in financially, Gratitude and giving thanks before and after receiving the money you truly desire is going to fasten up your desire and financial windfalls.

NOTE: "The best attitude is an attitude of gratitude"

Gratitude is the greatest and parent of all virtues. It is the grateful people who are always happy and attract more money into their respective lives.

Thanksgiving and praises open the infinite storehouse gate within us all for more abundance coming into our lives. *Gratitude attracts and complaints repel*. No new money-making ideas can come into your life unless you are grateful for what you already have.

The whole process of "Mind Power" to attract material gains and possessions can be summarized in one single word which is gratitude. A grateful heart never lacks anything including material money, cultivate the attitude of thanksgiving (gratitude) and you will never lack money and all the good things you truly deserve.

Lots and lots of people are kept in chains of poverty due to their lack of gratitude. These are the gratitude's affirmations for money as compiled by the author:

- ◆ I am grateful for my ever-increasing wealth and prosperity.
- ◆ I am grateful for the abundance of money on the way to me now.
- ◆ I am grateful that I have a wealthy mindset that attracts more money to me easily and effortlessly.
- ◆ I am grateful that I am always attracting unlimited money into my life with ease, comfort, joy, and love.
- ◆ I am grateful that I got passive income, coming to me regularly.
- ◆ I am grateful that money comes to me in increasing quantities through multiple sources and continuously.
- ◆ I am grateful for all the money I am receiving daily.
- ◆ I am grateful now that money is always coming into my experience easily and effortlessly.

NOTE: Always remember, a grateful heart is a strong magnet for miracles. Be grateful and always count your blessing one-by-one instead of misfortunes lacks and limitations. Don't worry about anything but in everything, through prayer and petition with thanks-giving, let your request be known to God (source of supplies) ", (Philippians 4:6).

"A GRATEFUL HEART IS A POWERFUL MAGNET FOR MIRACLES"

CHAPTER 9: MONEY AFFIRMATIONS

Affirmations are prayers, declarations, and an assertion that something exists and it's true. Take a statement, words, or auto-suggestions and keep repeating it constantly into your mind, that's an affirmation. Whatever statement or word that you keep repeating constantly to your mind habitually is going to end up provoking a feeling and therefore becoming your conditions and outer realities.

Affirmations or mantras are the principles of invoking the feeling of whatever realities you truly desire into your mind and therefore becoming your realities (condition). Invoke and invoke financial blessing and abundance into your subconscious mind every day and you will never lack material money".

Affirmations and chanting mantras is one of the easiest ways to attract money into your experience in life. This is a well-known method used by the ancient to get whatsoever they truly desire throughout the centuries.

These are some well-composed AFFIRMATIONS The Author is sharing with you to be, do and have all the good things you truly desire and all these affirmations are going to attract and draw more money into your pockets, hands, and bank accounts if you dare to use them habitually, positively and correctly. Speak them verbally and also believe the words as you are repeating them as often as you can to yourself in your mind.

- I love money and money loves me.
- I am a powerful money magnet.
- I am rich and wealthy.
- Money is my obedient faithful friend.
- I am always receiving money every day now.
- Money is the root of everything good to me personally.
- I am getting richer and richer every day.
- Money is abundant and it's on its way to me.
- I always have more than enough money to use and circulate.
- Expected and unexpected money comes to me now.
- The abundance of money flows to me now with ease, joy, and love.
- I am rich in good health, happiness, love, success, and unlimited money.
- I now live, feel and expect an abundance of money.
- I have a great relationship with money and money keeps blessing me.
- I am open and receptive to all the financial abundance the universe has for me, so that I may be able to give back even more to the world.
- I am attracting an endless abundance of money by keeping a gratitude mindset.
- Money keeps me economically healthy.
- Money always flows to me even when I sleep.

- Money flows easily and effortlessly freely into my bank account.
- I am using money to bless my life and other people's lives.
- I am focused on living a prosperous abundant rich Life.
- Money flows to me like a beautiful golden river.
- I am now permanently free of debts and any kind of money problems.
- I am a magnet of success and good fortunes.
- Everywhere I turn; here comes more money.
- I have a millionaire mindset; I think and feel like a millionaire; I am a millionaire.
- Abundance and lots of money are my birthrights and my natural state of mind.
- I am showing 100% gratitude's toward money, abundance, and the overflowing of wealth.
- I am forever rich.
- Big money is flowing into my life with ease and love.
- I am an irresistible powerful money magnet.
- I am a boss to money; money always obeys my command.
- People love giving me money.
- I feel rich and elegant.
- I am an energetic match to plenty of money.
- It is ok for me to be super-rich.
- I am a big-time moneymaker.
- I am using my wealth to enjoy and help others.

- My wealth network and net worth are forever increasing.
- God (source of supplies) give me money richly to enjoy and help others.
- I finally realized my dream of being a millionaire.
- I am always fascinated with more money making ideas.
- I see and feel more money pouring into my life in new exciting ways.
- I am the money man/lady.
- Money flows to me easily and naturally now.
- I release all the money blocks in my Subconscious mind now.
- Money can't just stay away from me.
- Money always finds her way around me.
- Everyone and everything prospers me now.
- Money comes to me as easy as I breathe.
- I am always walking in abundance of money.
- Money is attracted to me like bees to honey.
- All the money that I used and circulate comes back to me multiplied.
- I am a rich child of God and I have dominion over money.
- Poverty is foreign to my nature; I am Rich.
- My giving out money makes me wealthier.
- Everything I touch is minting money.
- I am laying up gold as dust.
- I am a custodian of money.
- I am rich in dollars, euros, pound sterling, and every coin of the realms.

- I am eternally wealthy.

    Thank you, God in me for the
    money.

"INVOKE AND INVOKE FINANCIAL BLESSINGS THROUGH AFFIRMATIVE PRAYER'S AND YOU WILL NEVER BE BROKE AND POOR."

CHAPTER 10: CONCLUSION

Now that the **"Secret Principles"** of attracting an abundance of money have been revealed to you in this book. It will be of an advantage for the readers to read and study this awesome volume several times as much as possible and apply all these "Principles" into your day to day daily routine to attract an abundance of money as you truly desire into your own experience by using the power of a made-up mind. Since you are also much more enlightened and fully aware of your God-given power knowing that money is in your mind, mouth, and consciousness.

Start using your almighty powers as revealed to you in the book and go ahead to start creating and manifesting the crab out of money like a natural-born moneymaker you truly are folks.

AFFIRM: "It is very easy for me to make money".

In conclusion, the author is sharing some of his favorite money quotes;

♦ "Money answers everything."
♦ "The secret of money is having some."
♦ "What money can't buy; I cannot use."
♦ "Those who say money can't buy happiness do not know where to shop."

- "Money is tied to a rich man's tongue."
- "The tongue of the rich is an abundance of money."
- "Money swore an oath, that who doesn't love her will never have her (Irish quote)."
- "Money is like dettol; it kills 99.9% of problems."
- "I hate math but I love counting money."
- "Money is sweeter than honey."
- "Money matters."
- "Money is not everything they say: but everything needs money."
- "Money isn't the most important thing in life, but its reasonably close to oxygen on the scale of preferences."
- "When money speaks: nobody checks the grammar."
- "Real money makers never run out of money because every day the government is printing."
- "Money is not the root of evil but poverty is."
- "Whoever has the money, makes the rules."
- "The tongue of the rich is money."
- "What did money say when everyone left? money said, "you can always count on me."
- "Money isn't everything in life but poverty is nothing."
- "Money is not everything but make sure you earn enough before speaking such nonsense."
- "Money doesn't make you happy they say, but it can park you right in front of a happy house."
- "Some say "money is the root of all evil"; but being poor is a damn shame."

- "Excuses are luxuries that the wealthy cannot afford."
- "When it comes to the question of money; everybody is of the same religion."
- "Money talks, things work."
- "Money makes a great sex appeal."

This book is to awaken, uplift, and empower the readers. Thank you for reading. – Emman Roberts a.k.a *'The money man'*.

ABOUT THE AUTHOR

Emman Roberts a.k.a **"the moneyman"** is an international author of self-help books using mind power and psychology of money to set the tone for his writing career to awaken, uplift, and empower the readers.

Emman is a strong believer in how to permanently eliminate and completely erase the idea of poverty out of the consciousness of mankind.

Peace, good health, happiness, love, prosperity, and more money.

ABOUT THE BOOK

Money is Looking for you will take you deeper into a **New World of financial Success, Prosperity, and Abundance of Money** beyond your fondest dreams.

It will give you more Mind-Blowing insight about manifesting more Financial Freedoms by using your Mind Powers to get more Green Powers (Money).

You are requested to diligently study and apply "**The Secret Principles**" as stated in the Book to draw an Abundance of Money into your experience and all the goods you truly desire.

REFERENCES

The holy bible; king James version

Revd. Ike (1982), a science of living study

guide; The good reads quotes

Pastor David Oyedepo (AZ Quotes)

CPSIA information can be obtained
at www.ICGtesting.com
Printed in the USA
BVHW041343150222
629075BV00012B/541

9 789692 292917